MESSAGES
FROM
SPIRIT

AN OPEN-AT-RANDOM
BOOK OF GUIDANCE

SYLVIA
BROWNE

st. lynn's
press

PITTSBURGH

Messages From Spirit
An Open-at-Random Book of Guidance

Copyright © 2009 by Sylvia Browne

ISBN-13: 978-0-9800288-6-7

Library of Congress Control Number: 2009924724
CIP information available upon request

First Edition, 2009

St. Lynn's Press • POB 18680 • Pittsburgh, PA 15236
412.466.0790 • www.stlynnspress.com

Typesetting & cover design—Holly Wensel, Network Printing Services
Editor—Catherine Dees

Printed in the United States of America
on recycled paper

This title and all of St. Lynn's Press books may be purchased for educational, business, or sales promotional use. For information please write:
Special Markets Department • St. Lynn's Press • POB 18680 • Pittsburgh, PA 15236

10 9 8 7 6 5 4 3 2 1

MESSAGES
FROM
SPIRIT

AN OPEN-AT-RANDOM
BOOK OF GUIDANCE

SYLVIA
BROWNE

To My Life Partner:

WILLIAM MICHAEL ULERY

❧

INTRODUCTION

꘏

This book is a gift of love, not just from me to you, but a gift to yourself and God. Take a page each day, read it and contemplate it for the day. By doing this, we also confirm and augment our soul to keep our soul in a positive mode rather than in a negative one. In this world, which is where hell is, it is important to keep good thoughts and do positive affirmations regularly. Some of these thoughts or sayings are to keep your thoughts upward. You may add to them by giving your own spin on your life or even by opening your soul mind to other possibilities. Sometimes the hardest things can be solved with a positive thought that may have skirted our minds; but when you see it in print, it brings a solution into focus. So use a page a day and by the end of the week you will find yourself walking a little taller, your head held high and with new or renewed conviction that will expand your soul.

A soul that never ventures out of the box that it has built for itself will lie dormant. Like our body if it doesn't move, the soul gets lazy and eventually the physical mind can even shut down. Use the messages in this book to find joy in the existence you and God decided on for your own perfection, and as I stated earlier, you will start feeling and looking better with each new day. Life is hard, we know that, but we also can have joy. So rather than being a victim or a martyr, let's begin to embrace joy and knowledge each day.

God love you.
I do,

Sylvia

DON'T LOOK FOR A
LAKE WHEN YOU ARE
STANDING IN A STREAM.

L ook to what you have around you and be grateful, instead of searching for more.   All you take with you when you leave this world is love, friendship, and good deeds.

IF MY ANTENNAS
ARE BENT, I MAY GET
GARBLED SIGNALS.

Every morning when you get up, ask God to keep your channel pure. God gave every one of us a cell phone. We just dropped it. Keep your mind quiet and listen and you'll hear God.

ALL CREATURES ARE DIVINE.
SOME JUST WEAR DIFFERENT
TRAPPINGS.

We have to stop being critical of people's color, creed, or sexuality. God made everyone and everything.

ANGER AND HATE MEAN WE DO
NOT LOVE OURSELVES.

Do not allow someone to disturb our inner soul's quiet grace. We have to make an effort to look Beyond and love our soul so that no one can hurt or disturb our peace.

How we treat others is how we treat God.

If we understand that each one of us is the spark of the Divine, we will be kinder and more caring to our fellowman and woman.

WHEN WE ARE IN THE
PRESENCE OF GREATNESS
WE HAVE A SENSE
OF SECURITY.

WHEN WE ARE IN THE
PRESENCE OF DARKNESS
WE HAVE A SENSE
OF UNEASINESS.

We should always take our first impression. If we meet someone and a small alarm goes off – run. Darkness pulls us down. Lights lifts us up to God.

IF ALL THE WORDS
EVER WRITTEN WERE
WRAPPED INTO A BALL,
THEY WOULD NOT OUTWEIGH
ONE WORD — LOVE.

The word love is synonymous with God, because God is all love and all forgiveness. God is constant and loves us unconditionally.

I WANT TO DRINK
THE WINE OF LIFE,
BUT I DON'T INTEND TO
GET INTOXICATED
BY IT — NOR ADDICTED
TO IT EITHER.

The Greeks say everything in moderation, but watch carefully that your soul doesn't get addicted to greed.

EVERYONE HAS A CLOSED
DOOR INSIDE.
ONLY GOD
CAN OPEN THAT DOOR.

Ask every night and morning that God open your soul's mind to the wonders that are all around. You'll see everything of beauty.

IN MEDITATION
YOUR SOUL GETS
A CHANCE TO GET A
WORD IN.

Our minds are so noisy and worrisome. Keep your mind quiet and you can hear the voice of God.

WE CAN ACCEPT RAIN,
BUT WE DON'T NEED
A FLOOD — SO ASK
GOD TO SHUT THE
WATER OFF.

It's true, God will not allow you to drown even though you have chosen your chart. You can still ask that the time of sorrow be shortened and that your soul get stronger from what you've been through.

I LOVE CHILDREN AND
ANIMALS BECAUSE
LIFE HASN'T CORRUPTED
THEM YET.

Often times when we grow up, we grow down in our thoughts and beliefs, and we don't see with innocent eyes. We make everything too complicated.

MY ONE PRAYER
EVERY MORNING
THAT HAS CARRIED
ME THROUGH MY LIFE
IS, "HI GOD, IT'S ME
AGAIN."

It doesn't matter how you pray. It can be just simply talking to God. Remember, God knows your heart and soul.

LOVE AND LOYALTY
ARE A FEW OF THE
PRIME VIRTUES,
BUT WE MUST REALIZE
WHEN THEY ARE
MISPLACED.

You can do as much as you can for another human being, but if they won't listen, you must walk away — because someone else will be waiting and be appreciative.

I WALK IN A MIST
OF MY OWN BIDDING
AND THAT'S WHY
I SEE DARKLY.

My guide Francine says, you only see the "light" when you climb the mountain of self, and that helping others makes the climb down easier.

Why toot your own horn?
If you are good enough,
someone else will
play it for you
and play it on key.

Is there anything more irritating than people who have the misfortune of feeling they are entitled? We can only earn respect and love. We are not entitled to anything we don't work for.

WE ALL WANT
TO MAKE A MARK
ON LIFE,
NOT A SCAR.

Take stock of your life and be conscientious about how you help and give, rather than being violent, surly, and in a bad mood.

I HOPE WHEN I
FINALLY PUNCH OUT,
MY SOUL CARD WILL
HAVE A LOT OF
OVERTIME ON IT.

Living life is hard, but we can make it easier by giving of ourselves – not just money but time. Relying on oneself to accomplish what we want is a greater gift than depending on others.

TEARS OF FRUSTRATION
ARE GOOD. FOR ONE
THING, THEY CLEAN
YOUR EYES OUT.

Instead of being frustrated, encounter the problem head-on and stick to your goals; otherwise you will live a life of quiet desperation.

LIVE EACH DAY
AS YOUR LAST,
AND TOMORROW
IS FOREVER.

To live in the now takes practice, but it's all we have. If you enjoy the now, tomorrow becomes a joy. Just make sure you are happy in the now.

IF YOU ARE NOT
COMMITTED,
YOU HAVE NO
PASSION
IN LIFE.

By not committing to life, love, family, or whatever aspect it may be, you will just waste your life and go off track.

STORE UP YOUR
TREASURE IN THE BOOK
ON THE OTHER SIDE.
DEPOSIT, DON'T
WITHDRAW.

Your actions toward others are your bank deposit. It's easy to be good to nice people, but try to be caring to everyone. It is a test.

ONE THING ABOUT DEATH,
YOU COME OUT OF IT
ALIVE.

We have it all backwards. When we come into life, we die, because we leave home to come down to this hell to learn for God.

IF LIFE GIVES YOU
CROWDS OF PEOPLE,
HAVE A PARTY.

Sometimes we can get overdone with people. Take time off, then invite your friends for a party so they don't feel neglected. Then you have seen them all and still have time to yourself.

THE CHILD IN ME
SEES AND KNOWS.
THE ADULT IN ME
CLOUDS THE ISSUE.

When we are young, we believe, and we are innocent; and then the world crowds in. Be more childlike.

THE OLD EXPRESSION,
"WATER SEEKS ITS OWN LEVEL"
APPLIES IN LIFE.

When we are confronted with darkness, we should run, because it can cause depression and illness. Greatness empowers us and lifts us up to God.

LIFE IS A GIFT
TO PERFECT.
THOSE WHO DON'T
SEE THIS
ARE TAKERS.

Life is a gift that we chose to advance our soul's perfection for God. As hard as it is, it is an opportunity to learn and expand our souls.

Instead of putting
satan (who doesn't
exist anyway)
or negativity
behind us, why not
put ourselves
behind us?

Instead of looking for the negativity and Satan that churches constructed, just stay away from dark-souled entities, and put love of people before yourself.

GUILT IS A CAGED ANIMAL THAT CAN'T GET OUT.

You can only have guilt if you meant harm, and most good souls only have guilt after the fact. So drop the guilt and go on with life.

As you travel along
your life's path,
try to carve out
one of joy and happiness.

That doesn't mean we don't grieve or feel sorrow at times, but if these feelings go on for too long, they make a rut in your soul that's hard to crawl out of.

I BELIEVE
IN
BELIEF.

People who say they don't believe usually are the ones that want irrefutable proof that God exists. They try so hard that it almost belies the fact that they are searching.

WHEN I MEDITATE,
I CONCENTRATE.
I WANT TO
CONCENTRATE
ON MY
MEDITATION.

You don't have to spend hours meditating. In the morning, I ask God to surround all my loved ones with the white light of the Holy Spirit and ask God to keep my channel pure.

NEVER LET
ANYONE PUT
THEIR BELIEFS
ON YOU.

Our Lord said we are temples, so seek and you will find your way to God on your own terms, because God understands everything.

NOTHING
IS GREATER THAN
LOVE.

Love is God. Love is forever and unconditional. Love is kind and forgiving and all encompassing Without love, your life is a dark shell.

NEVER BE BACKWARD
ABOUT GOING
FORWARD.

How bad can it be if you take a chance in life? If you don't go out on a limb, you will never see the view. Find your passion in life and go for it. Your passion is catching, and if you believe in you, so will others.

ONLY BY CONTRAST
OF SORROW
DO WE APPRECIATE
JOY.

If life was all pleasure, what would we learn or how would we grow spiritually?

KINDNESS SEEMS
TO COME IN SMALL
DOSES.
ANGER AND HATE
CAN FILL UP
A ROOM.

We have to realize this is a negative planet and negativity travels faster than positive energy. So use kindness frequently, and this positive energy will come back to you.

LOYALTY IS ONLY
WARRANTED
IF IT'S
RETURNED.

So many times we feel guilty about not being loyal, but look closely and see if it's returned. If not, then you owe nothing.

GRATITUDE

IS A

LEARNED

GIFT.

We don't have DNA in our make-up to be grateful. It is a learned ability that feels good when you are given something freely.

I WON'T JUST TRY,
I CAN DO IT.

Don't use the word, "try." It's too open ended. When you know you can, that's determination, and you will succeed.

WHEN YOU ENCOUNTER SOMEONE YOU DON'T FEEL GOOD ABOUT — RUN!

Too many times we don't take our first impression, and that is the most valid one from God. You may be encountering a dark soul entity. Better to be safe than sorry.

SMILES ARE THE
ONLY WINDOWS THAT
SHOW OUR SOULS
ARE CENTERED.

If you don't have smiles or find humor in your life, your spirituality is dying.

I DON'T WANT TO
CULTIVATE THE WHOLE WORLD —
I'M HAVING A HECK OF A TIME
KEEPING THE WEEDS
OUT OF MY OWN GARDEN.

It's important to take care of your own life before you venture out to save everyone else. You don't starve your family to feed your neighbors.

IF YOU ALWAYS LOOK DOWN,
YOU WILL ONLY SEE CRACKS,
CREVICES, AND DIRT.

If you look up, you see the stars, and if you are positive, good things come. If you are negative, you will attract crisis.

EVERY DAY
I SAY, "DEAR GOD,
THIS DAY IS FOR YOU."

It's great to pray, but remember that God knows your chart and what we are about. Acknowledge God. God doesn't need it. We do.

DON'T FEAR DEATH, BECAUSE YOU *ARE* DEAD, AND YOU CAME DOWN TO LEARN UNTIL YOU GO HOME AND REALLY LIVE.

Living forever is for the Other Side. When we are born, we come to learn and experience for God. When we die, we live for eternity with our loved ones and with our pets in God's love, and our souls expand from all the lessons we have learned.

My soul doth magnify
the lord even if
it's a bad day,
and I can only
bring up a droplet
of kindness.

Some days are better than others. Sometimes it's easy to be kind when we are having a good day. The real test is to give kindness when you don't feel like it.

WHAT DIFFERENCE
DOES IT MAKE WHAT
WE CALL GOD?
HE AND SHE KNOW
WHO THEY ARE.

It doesn't matter what creed or religion we are, as long as we know we are all going to the same place.

THERE IS NO HELL
EXCEPT THE ONE WE
MAKE FOR OURSELVES
ON THIS SIDE WHERE
NEGATIVITY EXISTS.

This is the only hell there is, and how we get through it is by loving God, doing good, and keeping it simple.

To love and be
abandoned leaves
a hole in your soul.

We should look at this abandonment as a blessing, as hard as it is, because after every bad experience, your soul prepares for God – if you don't crawl into that hole.

WHAT DO YOU LOVE IN LIFE?
WRITE OUT YOUR LOVES
AND GRATITUDES.

Concentrate on what you love rather than what you hate, because hate brings on illness. It eats you alive and lowers your immune system.

WHERE DOES YOUR
SPIRITUALITY LIE?
WHAT DO YOU BELIEVE IN?
IF IT'S ONLY IN A HIGHER
POWER, THAT'S ENOUGH.

To even believe that there is a being higher than you makes life easier, and the more you address it, the higher your soul rises — because unhappiness comes from the root of no belief.

THERE ARE MANY LOVES
IN LIFE.
SO INSTEAD OF LOOKING
FOR THE "ONE,"
SPEND YOUR TIME
IN LOVING.

If you look too hard, you send out a desperate energy. If you are in love with your family, friends and animals, you set yourself up for love to come to you.

DO NOT LET GUILT
OR WHAT COULD HAVE BEEN
RULE YOUR LIFE.

Guilt is a killer of spirituality. You wrote your chart, and you would have done the same thing over again. Leave it behind and be the better for the lesson.

IF YOU HAVE LIVED
THROUGH ABUSE, IT TRULY
IS A TERRIBLE EXPERIENCE —
BUT WORK THROUGH IT
WITH GOD'S HELP,
AND THEN GO ON
WITH LIFE.

Too many times we live with all our old memories and hurts, and let goodness walk by. Don't own your pain and suffering, because it begins to identify you.

DON'T HAVE FEAR
OF ALONENESS OR LONELINESS.
YOU MUST REALIZE YOU
ARE SURROUNDED BY ANGELS
AND YOUR GUIDES AND
YOUR PASSED LOVED ONES.

If you stay alone and don't activate, you will live out your self-fulfilled prophecy. Take a class, join a church, activate. You are surrounded by loved ones.

FEAR OF DEATH
IS THE FEAR OF THE
UNKNOWN AND
THE FEAR THAT
WE WILL CEASE
TO BE.

There is no such thing that we won't still exist on the Other Side or live another life. God didn't make us to destroy us.

I AM THE CENTER
OF MY UNIVERSE, AND
I AM A SPARK OF
THE DIVINE SPARKLER.

This doesn't mean you have a false ego. The "I am" is just knowing you are, and having joy in the fact that you are truly the offspring of God.

IF YOU FEEL YOU
ARE IN A DESERT PERIOD,
JUST PLOW THROUGH IT.
YOU WILL COME TO
THE END OF IT.

Everyone goes through what I call a "desert period" where you just survive life. But realize that during this time you learn endurance, patience, and survival. The more you accept it, the sooner it ends.

I WILL ASK
MOTHER GOD
TO SEND ABUNDANCE
AND FINANCIAL GAIN.

If you ask Mother God, regardless what it is, there is a 90% chance She answers. Maybe not in the way you thought, but the answer comes. Remember to share abundance.

PHOBIAS ARE ONLY
THE CRIES OF THE
SOUL TO BE LISTENED
TO FROM PAST LIVES.

So many illnesses and phobias are the result of past-life cell memories or subconscious memories that you have carried over from a past life. Ask God every night to remove all negativity and put the white light of the Holy Spirit around you.

LIFE HAS GIANT
MOUNTAINS AND DEEP
VALLEYS AND MEADOWS.

If we don't have the hard climbs, then how do we appreciate the valleys and streams and lovely meadows of life?

I CANNOT IDENTIFY
MYSELF BY MY ABUSES
OR ILLNESSES. THESE
ARE MY TEXT BOOKS
OF LEARNING.

You are not the car you drive. If your engine goes bad, that's not you. Your body is only like the car you drive — it is not you.

EACH DAY WITHOUT
A GOOD ACT IS
A DAY LOST.

How much does it take to call a sick friend or let someone go in front of you in line? Too much time is wasted with long idle periods.

IF YOU ARE FRANTIC
ABOUT LOVE AND HAPPINESS,
THE STRESS OF IT
WILL CAUSE THESE
TO ELUDE YOU.

If you are quiet in your soul and wipe the frantic negativity away, love and happiness will find you.

LOVE GOD.
DON'T FEAR GOD,
BECAUSE GOD
IS ALL LOVE.

Two emotions cannot occupy the mind at the same time, so if you fear, you cannot love.

IT DOESN'T MATTER
IF YOU DON'T
BELIEVE IN GOD.
GOD STILL BELIEVES
IN YOU.

An atheist is a person crying out for proof, and yet it is sitting in the soul to be listened to.

Don't fear
hell or death.
You are already
in it.

The reason you don't need to fear it is because you are already in hell here on earth, and this is death, and the Other Side is life.

YOU CAN BE
AS SICK AS YOU
WANT TO BE, OR
AS WELL AS YOU
WANT TO BE.

When you feel you are getting sick or are already sick, scream in your mind, "NO!" The mind is the killer and the healer.

GERMS DON'T MAKE
YOU SICK,
PEOPLE DO.

When you first meet someone, take your first impression. It is the truest and most valid. Constantly being around negative people over a period of time can make you physically ill. Make a list of all the people in your life. If you find someone who makes you feel tired, etc., then drop them.

WE SHOULD WANT
TO GO TO GOD
AND SAY WE DID IT
ALL ON OUR OWN.

Too many people want something for nothing. Everything in life comes with a price. There are no free rides.

YOU WILL NEVER
HAVE A FRIEND
IF YOU
ARE NOT ONE.

So many people feel alone, but they don't take stock of the fact that they are not kind or approachable.

ASK NOT WHO WILL LOVE YOU. ASK WHO YOU CAN LOVE.

When you are in the state of loving, love will be attracted to you. We attract what we feel and who we are.

To be really wise,
be an observer
of life and people.

You can read every book that was ever written, but if you are not an observer or a participant in life, you will be dull and boring.

IF WE FIND SOME THINGS
THAT ARE TOO HARD
TO FORGIVE,
GIVE THEM TO GOD.

To forgive is divine. We are part of the Divine, but we have not reached our ultimate divinity yet. What is too hard to forgive should be given to God, and in His and Her divineness, they will be lifted from you.

MY GRANDMOTHER
USED TO SAY,
"SMILE AND THE WORLD
SMILES WITH YOU,
CRY TOO MUCH
AND YOU'LL CRY ALONE."

This doesn't mean we can't ventilate, but when we become a victim and a martyr, people get tired of your negativity. Leave it behind and live for today and tomorrow, not yesterday.

TIME IS TOO PRECIOUS
TO WASTE ON NEGATIVITY,
HATE, BIGOTRY, AND
THE FEELING OF ENTITLEMENT.

Time is fleeting and when it's gone, you can never get it back. Why not spend time on the joy of the moment instead of what was or what could have been.

LOVE IS THE MOST
WRITTEN ABOUT SUBJECT.
POETS, PLAYWRIGHTS, AUTHORS,
ETC. AND YET, IT SEEMS
EVERYONE STILL SEARCHES
FOR THE PERFECT LOVE.

Only God is the perfect love. God's love is never critical, always constant, and unconditional.

FEAR IS A DEFINITE
SIGN OF YOUR NOT HAVING FAITH
IN YOURSELF AND ALSO
FAITH IN GOD.

Fear of the unknown shouldn't scare you, because God and your angels always have an escape hatch for you, and as I've said, out of every bad comes good if you look for it.

ANIMALS ARE GOD'S GIFT
TO HUMANKIND,
SO SHOW THEM
UNCONDITIONAL LOVE.

We can learn a lot from animals. They don't care what we do or what we look like. They just love us unconditionally.

YEARS AGO
WHEN I LOST A LOVE
THE WORLD SEEMED DIRTY.

When sadness hits, we feel everything is bad, and then one day if we open our hearts, love heals and we can see and smell the roses again.

AS BAD AS TODAY WAS,
AND IT WAS ROUGH . . .

I had a late lecture night, my plane was late, luggage problems, hotel not ready. When I arrived, I was a mess! In the midst of all this, a woman walked up to me before I got on the elevator, grabbed my hand, and said I saved her life.

Suddenly, all the irritation left and I felt instantly lighter. Truly there is a silver lining in each difficult circumstance.

I HATE THE PHRASE
THAT NO GOOD DEED
GOES UNPUNISHED.
WHOEVER WROTE THAT
WAS A MISERABLE
PERSON.

Every good deed goes into the Hall of Records, and it's always rewarded by another good deed, and not always from the same source.

PEOPLE ASK ME,
"WHAT IS GOD?"
WELL, MY GUIDE SAYS,
FATHER GOD IS A
REAL PERSONAGE,
JUST LIKE MOTHER GOD.

The one thing, though, is that God the Father can't hold a visage or an image very long. He is too powerful and His energy is too vast, but everyone on the Other Side can feel Him always.

YOU CAN GO TO
ANY CHURCH OR HAVE
ANY BELIEF, BECAUSE
GOD IS ALL THE SAME
EVERYWHERE.

Remember, though, anywhere can be a church, because you are a temple. God doesn't make junk.

A WOMAN APPROACHED ME
IN THE AIRPORT AND ASKED,
"AREN'T YOU...?"
I FINISHED IT BY SAYING,
"YES, I AM SYLVIA BROWNE."
SHE REPLIED, "NO, THAT'S
NOT RIGHT."

Really, as Shakespeare said, 'What's in a name?' I replied, "You're right. I work at Starbucks." She then gave a nod of recognition.

———————————— ࣷ ————————————

IT AGGRAVATES ME WHEN
PEOPLE IN THE PUBLIC EYE
WANT THEIR PRIVACY.
IF THAT'S THE CASE, THEY
SHOULD KEEP THEIR FACES OFF
TELEVISION OR THE SCREEN.
THE GENERAL PUBLIC
ARE THE ONES
WHO MADE THEM
FAMOUS.

W hat kind of, and notice I say "false ego," do these people have that makes them think they are entitled? I hate entitlement.

PEOPLE OFTEN WANT
TO WIN THE LOTTERY
OR GET MONEY
HANDED TO THEM.

W on't it feel good to stand in front of God and say, "I did it all, Lord, on my own."

SET YOUR ALARM
15 MINUTES BEFORE
YOU HAVE TO GET UP,
AND LET YOUR MIND FLOW
AND GO TO THE
OTHER SIDE.

The Aborigines call this the "dreamtime," and it brings them closer to God.

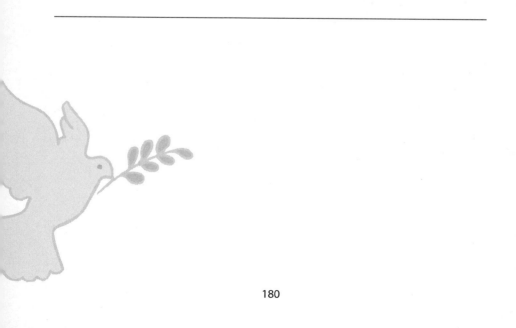

OUR LORD WANTS US TO BE
HIS FRIEND AND HE OURS.

Sadly, we have placed Him so far above us that we can't reach Him, and that wasn't His message.

THE CHILD IN ME WANTS
MY WAY.
THE ADULT IN ME
KNOWS BETTER.

Both sides of us are great. Never lose your childlikeness or your maturity. Otherwise, you lose God.

WHEN WE DIE,
WE ARE BORN.
WHEN WE ARE BORN,
WE DIE.

This makes sense, because this life is transient, and the Other Side is home and eternity.

THE HOLE WE SOMETIMES FEEL

IN OUR STOMACH IS

REALLY HOMESICKNESS.

We come into life missing home and we don't have a way back again until it's our time to leave this life.

THERE ISN'T
FATE OR KISMET.

The only thing that exists is the chart you wrote on the Other Side – and when the time comes, everything lines up.

CELEBRATE YOUR BODY
AND BE GRATEFUL FOR
ALL THE GOOD AND THE BAD.

If you don't appreciate you body, your temple, then other people sense this and will point out your flaws.

FEAR CAN COME FROM
AN UNREALIZED DREAM
OR A STOPPING OF SOMETHING
YOU WANTED TO DO.

R ather than looking at fear as a bad feeling, look at it as an alarm telling you that you weren't supposed to do something.

EVERY DAY WHEN YOU GET UP,
DON'T LET ONE
NEGATIVE THOUGHT
COME IN.

Negative thoughts will undoubtedly try to break through, but each time they do, immediately banish them.

EVERY BAD THING
THAT OCCURS
IS THE BEGINNING
OF A NEW GRAND THING
TO COME.

People get so caught up in the bad, they miss all the good that goes by.

I DON'T WANT MY MIND
TO BE FILLED WITH A
TORNADO OF THOUGHTS
AND DECISIONS.

Quiet your mind and ask the Holy Spirit to send a breeze that gets rid of negativity.

WHY DO YOU THINK
THEY CALL GRANDPARENTS
GRAND?
BECAUSE THEY ARE!

Grandparenting is easier because you don't have to worry about everything the way parents do. You can just enjoy the children as God's gift.

I WANT A LANTERN
IN MY SOUL
THAT NEVER
GOES OUT.

L et your soul's light be a beacon for anyone in darkness who needs help.

SOMETIMES WE FEEL
AS IF WE ARE IN A PLAY,
BUT THERE ARE PAGES
OF THE SCRIPT
MISSING.

When this happens, stand still until time and the other players catch up to you, and then you will find your place.

I LOVE BECAUSE I NEED.
I NEED BECAUSE I LOVE.

We should love not just out of need for need's sake, but because you want to love.

GRIEF IS A DRAGON
THAT RISES UP
IN THE STOMACH,
AND YOU FEEL AS IF
IT WILL EAT YOUR HEART.

When grief hits, just remember we all meet together on the Other Side.

PEOPLE ASK IF THEIR
LOVED ONES ARE HAPPY
ON THE OTHER SIDE.

If people weren't happy on the Other Side, it would be hell, like it is here. Everyone is happy there.

IT DOESN'T MATTER
IF YOU FEEL
GOD DOESN'T LOVE YOU
OR FORGIVE YOU.

Y ou have to forgive yourself, because God has forgiven
you and loves you no matter what.

I CAN'T UNDERSTAND
HOW I LOVED YOU
SO MUCH AND
YOU DECEIVED ME.

It isn't your fault if someone you love and thought you knew changes. You have to go on and think of Our Lord as the ultimate lover.

I DON'T NEED TO PRAY
FOR GOD,
BUT FOR ME TO BRING ME
CLOSER TO GOD.

God always knows our hearts, but prayer affects us so we spiritually grow and bring our souls closer to God.

ABOUT THE AUTHOR

ylvia **Browne,** author of *Life on the Other Side*, and *If You Could See What I See*, is a world renowned spiritual teacher, psychic, author and researcher in the field of parapsychology. A prolific writer with over 48 published works, Sylvia is known for her dynamic, genuine, down-to-earth style and personality. Some of her other best loved books are *Contacting Your Spirit Guide*, *Psychic Healing*, *Secret Societies*, *Spiritual Connections*, and *All Pets Go To Heaven*. In the years since she first manifested her psychic ability at the age of three, she has helped thousands of people gain control of their lives, live more happily, understand the meaning of life, and find God in their own unique way.

Sylvia's philosophy of life is based upon research into past lives, via hypnosis and through the information obtained through her deep trance channeling ability. In 1986, she founded the Society of Novus Spiritus (meaning New Spirit) based upon a Christian Gnostic theology. Her goals are to give aid to the infirm, shelter to the homeless, and establish a spiritual community that loves God (both the Father and Mother God) without the sin and guilt found in most of today's faiths.

She lives in Northern California with her husband, Michael Ulery.

Sylvia can be reached online at *www.sylvia.org*.